The Funeral Service

Service at the Funeral Home

_____
Funeral Home

_____
date   hour

Service at the Church

_____
Church

_____
Officiating

_____
date   hour

Service at the Cemetery

_____
Cemetery

_____
date   section   lot

"God shall wipe away all tears from their eyes"

Revelation 21:4

FAMILY

father _____

mother _____

father's father _____

father's mother _____

mother's father _____

mother's mother _____

OTHER MEMBERS OF THE FAMILY

_____

_____

_____

_____

_____

Foreword

EVERY GREAT SORROW ravages the soul with its own particular sadness. But what sadness can compare with that sense of utter desolation that consumes us when we suffer the loss of a loved one? It is too deep for tears; too numbing to let the kindness and sympathy of our friends ease our grief and loneliness. Later, the tears will come; later, the kindness and sympathy will help. But for the moment we remain alone in our sorrow; we feel lost and abandoned in this, our time of supreme need.

But we are not really alone, not really abandoned. For though we may remain beyond the reach of human consolation Jesus, now, more than at any other time, draws near and offers His help. In His infinite love and compassion He yearns to come and abide with us, bringing that understanding and consolation that He alone can bestow at such a time. We need only open wide our grief-stricken hearts to the Master and welcome Him in.

Now His timeless message is our greatest need. Now we must listen to His words as we have seldom, perhaps never, listened before. Others, though anxious to help, can do no more than commiserate with us in our grief. He alone can give us strength and lift up our hearts with His truth.

"Come unto me," He whispers to us, "and I will give you rest." If we respond to His loving invitation, allowing His divine wisdom to pierce the heavy sadness that curtains our souls, we will receive the sweet rest and refreshment He has promised. Now He will teach us personally the very core of His message to mankind. Now when our bereavement has emptied our hearts of all else, He will teach us the true meaning of life and the true meaning of suffering and the true meaning of death.

As we listen to Him and learn this great truth our present suffering will not, indeed, vanish. Jesus' message is no mere placebo. He will open our eyes to much wider spiritual horizons and teach us to see our bereavement in a new and proper perspective. As our spiritual vision grows under the Master's instruction, the peace of Christ that surpasses understanding will slowly but surely replace the void in our hearts.

Taking us gently to Himself Jesus will quietly recall for us the message He taught by word and example while He was on earth. "Here, in this life," He will remind us, "you have no abiding city. You are a pilgrim passing through. You are journeying to your true home in heaven, and the signposts on this road are trials and sorrows and death."

Consider, for a moment, how vividly Jesus demonstrated this very truth by the example of His own life on earth. As God's own Son He could have chosen to live among men receiving nothing but the splendor and glory to which He, the King of Kings, had a right. Yet, what kind of life did He, in fact, choose for Himself?

He was born in an abandoned stable. While still a small child He became a displaced person in Egypt, whither His mother and Joseph fled with Him to protect Him from Herod's evil designs. Most of His remaining years on earth were lived in the obscurity of Nazareth. When, eventually, He emerged from his obscurity to begin preaching His message to mankind what was His experience? The majority of those to whom He preached rejected Him, or regarded Him as nothing more than a wonder-worker. Seldom did His miracles win belief in Him as the Messiah.

Even His closest followers frequently caused Him sorrow and deep disappointment. Judas betrayed Him for thirty pieces of silver. In the courtyard of Caiaphas' palace, while His enemies subjected Him to that travesty of justice they called a trial, Peter denied even knowing Him. Thomas refused to believe that He had risen from the dead.

Climaxing the sufferings and seeming-failure of His life on earth was His cruel death on the Cross. He had come among men to redeem them from sin and teach them the way of salvation. He went about doing good, lavishing His love and divine healing-power on the sick, the maimed and the dead. In return He was sentenced to a criminal's death. As He lay dying on the Cross the mockery of those He had come to help rang loudly in His ears.

This was the life that Jesus Christ freely chose for Himself. Thus did He gloriously match His deeds with His words, teaching us the true meaning of life and the true meaning of suffering and the true meaning of death. Thus did He teach us His great message. He, who could have chosen regal honors and unalloyed joy, chose instead hardship and suffering culminating in death by crucifixion.

On the Cross He used suffering and death to conquer sin, showing us that sin—not death—is the only true evil. Three days later He arose from the tomb, proving that death is but the gateway to a glorious new life for all who love and believe in Him.

Here is the very core of Christ's timeless message to mankind. Life's sufferings and frustations have a deep and rich meaning. Death is not the end. It is the beginning of an eternity of happiness for which our pilgrimage here on earth is but the preparation. Grasp this message now and our present sorrow will assume its true perspective. Ignore or reject it and life itself can only be meaningless.

As we ponder this great truth it may be helpful to recall an example with which everyone is familiar. All of us at one time or another have had occasion to admire the beauty and design of a fine piece of embroidery. Perhaps we turned the cloth over and looked at the underside of the embroidery. There, instead of beauty and design, we saw a meaningless chaos of threads seemingly running wild in their disorder.

But is this disorder? Is it really meaningless? A moment's reflection serves to remind us that it only seems to be so. Having seen the "right" side of the embroidery we know that the "wrong" side only appears to be meaningless. Without the "wrong side" the beauty and design of the "right" side could not exist.

Life, especially when we are bowed down under the burden of some great sorrow, often looks like the "wrong" side of embroidery. It seems to be nothing but a meaningless succession of frustrations and sorrows. But Jesus assures us that this side of life is not meaningless at all. His own life on earth was a glorious vindication of the purpose and meaningfulness of suffering and death. Likewise the suffering and death in our own lives are meaningful parts of God's total plan for mankind. Like the "wrong" side of embroidery they are needed to produce the finished pattern that God is designing for us.

We cannot, of course, turn life over like a piece of embroidery and see how the "wrong" side contributes to the beauty and design of the "right" side. Instead we turn to Jesus with faith, and learn from Him how the threads of suffering and death are woven by God into that beautiful pattern that is our final and everlasting destiny.

"Come unto me," Jesus calls to us, "and learn this lesson." In learning it we will find the hope and peace, the strength and inspiration that are the reward of all who set humbly at the feet of the Master and let Him teach them. Then we will be able to accept our present sorrow, and indeed all life's trials, with calm understanding and courage.

COME UNTO ME by Heinrich Hofmann

In a spirit of community service, we the following, and our employees, present this beautiful volume for your inspiration and consolation

ALTOONA FEDERAL SAVINGS & LOAN ASSOCIATION

BURKETT MOTORS
Bob Burkett

RUSSEL M. WEST
Russel M. West Insurance Agency

FISHER'S PHARMACY
John W. Bush, R.Ph.

TIMOTHY A. BERKEBILE FUNERAL HOME

BEDFORD,
PENNSYLVANIA

"THE PLAN OF THE MASTER WEAVER"

My life is but a weaving
    Between the Lord and me,
I may not choose the colors,
    He knows what they should be;
For He can view the pattern
    Upon the upper side
    While I can see it only
    On this, the under side.
Sometimes He weaveth sorrow,
Which seemeth strange to me;
But I will trust His judgment,
    And work on faithfully;
'Tis He who fills the shuttle,
And He knows what is best,
So I shall weave in earnest,
    Leaving to Him the rest.
Not till the loom is silent
And the shuttles cease to fly
Shall God unroll the canvas
And explain the reason why—
The Dark threads are as needed
    In the Weaver's skillful hand
As the threads of gold and silver
    In the pattern He has planned.

Come Unto Me

A story of timeless significance,
inspiring peace in the hearts of
all who grasp and live its meaning

Copyright © 1962, by

GOOD WILL PUBLISHERS, Inc.

Gastonia, North Carolina

Classic™ binding
R. R. Donnelley & Sons Company
patents--U.S. pending

The Lord is my Shepherd

The Lord is my shepherd; I shall not want.

He maketh me to lie down in green pastures: he leadeth me beside the still waters.

He restoreth my soul: he leadeth me in the paths of righteousness for his name's sake.

Yea, though I walk through the valley of the shadow of death, I will fear no evil: for thou art with me; thy rod and thy staff they comfort me.

Thou preparest a table before me in the presence of mine enemies: thou anointest my head with oil; my cup runneth over.

Surely goodness and mercy shall follow me all the days of my life: and I will dwell in the house of the Lord for ever.

The Life of Christ

[INTRODUCTION]

THE STORY of the life of Our Lord and Savior, Jesus Christ, on earth, is above and beyond all else, the account of His glorious triumph over suffering and death. Christ's message is timeless. It applies to the whole human race now, as it did when He lived and suffered here on earth, and as it will till the end of time.

The message of His life is one of hope and inspiration. The depth of this message, with all its help and strength, we, for the most part, never fully value or appreciate, till we ourselves are bowed down with sorrow and sadness. Then, if never before, we begin to realize our need for the kind of strength and courage that only Christ's words and example can implant in a human heart.

That there is a crying need for such strength and courage, in our present age, few will deny. Today, having set up comfort and convenience as our idols, most people tend to think of trials and suffering as the ultimate evil. Vast numbers, in our day, simply crumple at the approach of all kinds of fears, whether real or imaginary. Yet, only a generation ago, our forefathers, who meditated often on Christ's words and example, remained resolute and unbowed in face of hardship and disaster.

In this striking contrast there is surely a message for our age. Imbued with Christ's teachings, our forefathers lived by the wise conviction that suffering and sorrow are integral parts of life's normal pattern. Facing life with courage and hope, they knew that the conquest of life's trials, and even death, as Christ Himself has so clearly demonstrated, is the true test of a person.

In offering this Life of Christ, therefore, we trust that many will draw inspiration from His words and example, and learn that the victory of the spirit is life's greatest triumph. For, as millions have discovered, in every age, Christ's strength and help can enable us to live, amid life's greatest stress and suffering, with deep peace in our hearts.

Gabriel Appears to Mary

THE STORY of Our Lord Jesus Christ begins with a woman, for Our Lord was truly Man as well as God. The Virgin Mary was chosen from all time to have the greatest privilege a creature could enjoy.

Her privilege has been beautifully expressed by Wordsworth thus:

>"Mother, whose virgin bosom was uncrossed
>With the least shade of thought to sin allied,
>Woman, above all women glorified,
>Our tainted nature's solitary boast."

This was God's plan for her, but Mary had to wait for His appointed time to hear of it. She lived in the little town of Nazareth and was betrothed to one of her countrymen named Joseph. Both, though poor, were descended from the royal race of David. At God's appointed time, the angel Gabriel entered her home and announced to her God's plan.

The humble girl was puzzled and troubled by these words. The angel quickly reassured her however, and gently calmed her fears, before breaking the news. "Behold, thou shalt conceive in thy womb and shalt bring forth a Son, and thou shalt call his name Jesus. He shall be great and shall be called the Son of the Most High. . . ." To Mary, familiar with the prophecies of the Savior, this could mean only one thing: she was to become the mother of Christ.

Showing extraordinary prudence in the face of such astonishing news, Mary requested further explanation. She knew not man. In this wonderful girl there was not the slightest hint of prudery. Her holiness, like all true holiness, was sane, balanced and realistic. How then could she be a mother since she knew not man? The angel Gabriel, matching her frankness, then told her of the divine plan, which insured that she would be the mother of the Anointed One, yet remain a Virgin.

God planned His Son's birth in this marvelous way, showing us, once more, the depth of divine wisdom, so far beyond our understanding. God's ways are not our ways. In the midst of life's trials, this thought should always be with us, for in His Infinite Wisdom, God sees all and knows all. We can see but a little part of His plans. Knowing His Infinite Goodness, we can abandon ourselves to His love and find His peace that surpasses all understanding. In all things, God knows best.

GABRIEL APPEARS TO MARY by Bartolomé Esteban Murillo

Mary Visits Elizabeth

THE ANGEL Gabriel, in revealing to Mary the wondrous news that she was to be the Mother of God, had also told her that her cousin, Elizabeth, though advanced in years, would bear a son. This important link between the Savior and His herald, John the Baptist, was established even in the womb.

Setting out on the three days' journey, Mary hastened to her cousin's side. Entering the house of Elizabeth she greeted her, and immediately the infant John leaped in the womb. At that moment Mary's privilege was revealed to Elizabeth and she cried out with a loud voice: "Blessed art thou among women, and blessed is the fruit of thy womb. And whence is this to me, that the mother of my Lord should come to me?"

Mary, answering her cousin's congratulations, recited her song of thanksgiving. In this beautiful Hebrew poem she pours out the joy and thanks that have reigned in her heart since she received the wonderful news.

The Jews learned many passages of the Scriptures by heart, and the public reading of the Sacred Books in the synagogue familiarized them further with these passages. And so in her canticle of joy the inspired words come easily to Mary's lips.

Mary's thanksgiving song foretells the Kingdom that her Son would establish, and expresses her deep humility that she should be chosen as mother of such a King. His Kingdom would, most surely, upset all worldly values. For hate He would replace with love, pride with humility and greed with a generous spirit. His Kingdom would not be of this world. The proud and mighty, then, trusting in the things of this world would find this King contemptuous of their influence and material possessions. The lowly and hungry, on the other hand, would find themselves the focus of His mercy and goodness.

We should often pause to think of this great truth: Christ's Kingdom is not of this world. Frequently in life we lose touch with this thought and regard the things of this world as ends in themselves. Consequently we worry and sorrow over things that have no lasting value. Losing the true perspective, in this way, we allow trivial things to assume a false importance and exact from us heartache far beyond their due.

After a three months' stay with Elizabeth, Mary bade her farewell and returned home. She had much to attend to, in preparation for the greatest birth of all time. Joseph, her betrothed, had to learn of her miraculous conception. Mary had full confidence that though her condition must puzzle this just man, God would settle his doubts by revealing to him her exalted privilege.

MARY VISITS ELIZABETH by Carl Bloch

The Birth of Christ

Shortly after Mary's return from her cousin's home, the simple marriage ceremony, conducted according to Jewish custom, was completed, and Joseph led his bride to his own home, where they began their married life.

The Roman Emperor, Augustus, issued an edict that all his subject peoples register in their city of origin. The family of Joseph originated in Bethlehem, so he was obliged to make the journey there from Nazareth. Though knowing her time was near at hand, Mary, with utter trust in God, set out with him on this arduous journey. Bethlehem was, understandably, overcrowded, since many visitors had arrived for the registration. Consequently, the only shelter Joseph could find for his wife was a little stable, probably owned by the people who conducted the inn, where they had sought admission in vain. Here in this lowly shelter, Mary brought forth the King of Kings. A cold drafty stable became the center of the universe.

God had arranged that His Son be paid homage, just after His birth, by those very dear to Christ's heart. We shall see that throughout His life, the poor and the humble were especially favored. As Mary and Joseph, rapt in loving devotion, bent over the Child, an angel announced the great news to a group of shepherds nearby. These tidings were not revealed to the great ones of Israel, the priests, the scholars, the Pharisees. The poor, humble, sincere shepherds were the favored ones. A chorus of angels thrilled them with their song proclaiming glory to God in heaven and peace to men on earth. Full of faith the shepherds hastened to the stable and adored the God-child, then fled to their humble homes to tell their families of the wonders they had witnessed.

The surroundings of poverty and discomfort that God chose for the birth of His Son must surely carry for us all an important message. Consistently Our Lord would teach, by word and example, the necessity of self-denial. So from His first moment on earth He would show us that though He might have chosen splendor and luxury, He chose a borrowed stable for His birth, as at death He chose a borrowed grave.

In these ways Christ showed us, by His example, even from the first moment of His birth, that the truly spiritual person will choose self-denial rather than the soft comforts of life. Ease and self-indulgence are the poorest possible preparation for bearing the daily crosses which His followers are asked to support patiently.

THE BIRTH OF CHRIST by J. L. Lund

The Presentation in the Temple

ON THE EIGHTH DAY following His birth, the Divine Child submitted in utter humility to the Jewish ceremony of circumcision, shedding the first drops of that blood, which would eventually flow on Calvary as a cleansing torrent. Another strict requirement of the Jewish religion was that Jesus, the firstborn, be consecrated to God, and that Mary undergo the ceremony of purification. Neither He nor His mother was bound by these laws, but again setting us an example of complete obedience and humility they submitted to them.

Forty days after His birth, therefore, the Holy Family journeyed to Jerusalem for these ceremonies. The ceremony of Mary's purification took place in the morning. Being poor, Joseph would only be able to afford two pigeons or turtle doves, to be sacrificed by the priests, as a part of the ceremony of purification. The presentation of the Child was a much more simple ceremony and seems to have involved no further rite than the payment of five shekels to the priests.

While the Holy Family was still in the Temple, an event of deep significance took place linking once more the Old Dispensation with the New. Simeon, a just and devout man, in whose heart glowed an unshakable faith in the coming of the Savior, met Jesus, Mary and Joseph. Inspired by God, he immediately recognized Jesus as the Redeemer of Israel. Piously taking the Child from His mother's arms Simeon praised God "because my eyes have seen Thy salvation which Thou hast prepared before the face of all peoples." He then prophesied that this Child was set for the fall and rising of many. Clouding the joy, Simeon goes on to foretell the rejection of Christ by many, and warns Mary of the sword of suffering that will pierce her heart, as she shares the sufferings of her Son.

The sword of suffering, foretold for Mary, would be buried in His mother's heart all her life. Her mother's nature shrank from the pain and suffering her Son would endure. Yet, though human, just as we, she would bear it with resignation always, through faith and love of her Son. We, too, can bear that sharpest of all human sufferings—the sword that must be borne in the heart for a lifetime—and win calm resignation, through faith and the love of God.

Scarcely had Simeon finished speaking when Anna, a pious widow, devoted to the service of God, approached the little group, and, inspired as was Simeon, recognized the Divine Child as the Savior. Thus, for her too, did God fulfill a lifelong desire.

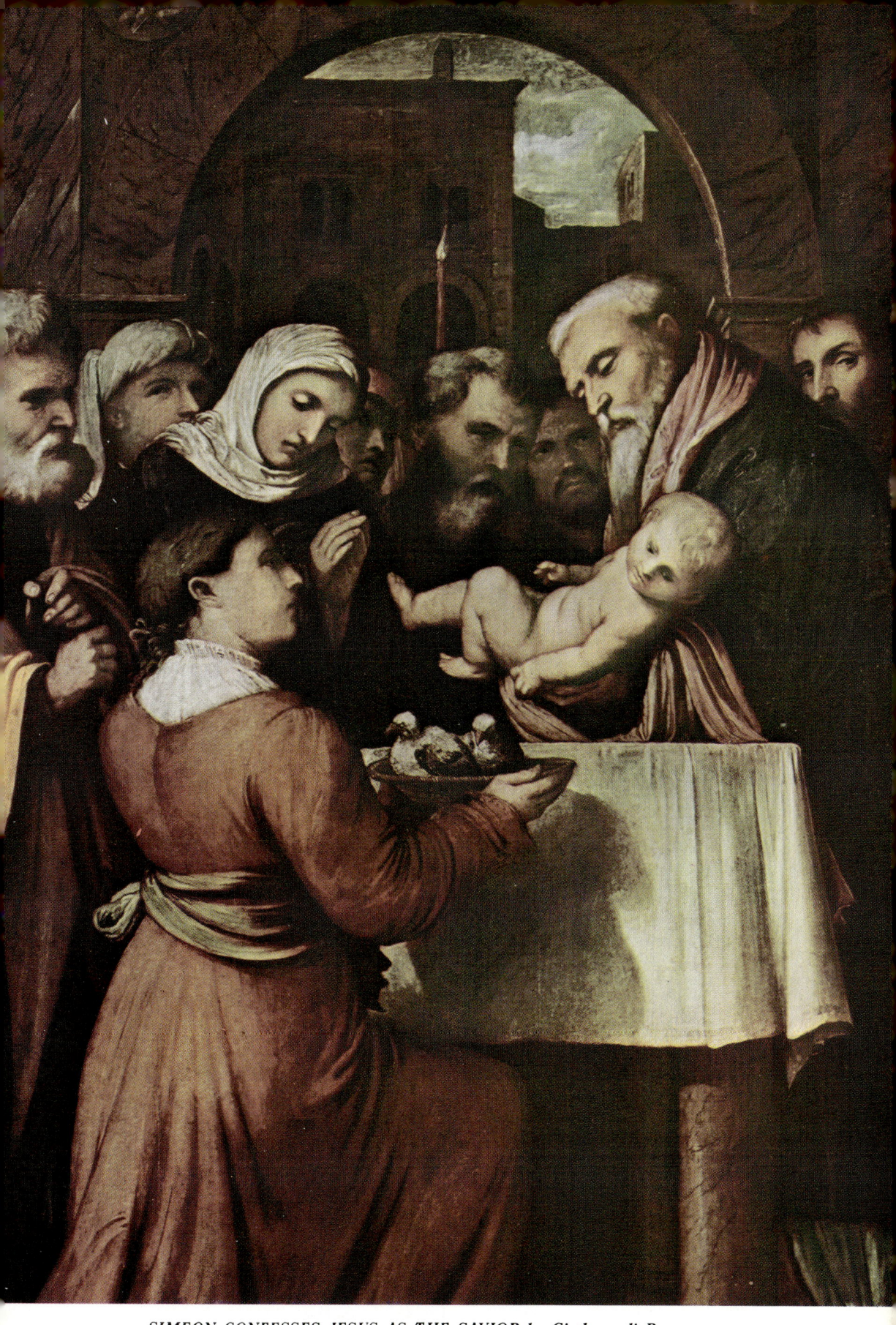

SIMEON CONFESSES JESUS AS THE SAVIOR by Girolamo di Romano

Adoration of the Wise Men

SINCE CHRIST was the King of Kings it was suitable that He should have recognition from representatives of the pagan world. And so Providence decreed that the Wise Men, scholar-priests of the Gentile world, led by the star, should come to Bethlehem to pay their respects, and adore their God.

This phenomenon of the star which traced a path for the wise men of the East to Bethlehem, is but another of the wonders with which God studded the lifetime of His Son on earth.

Following the star, the Wise Men proceeded to the capital city, Jerusalem, confident of gathering there reliable information. Their simple question "Where is He that is born King of the Jews?" created great excitement. King Herod, a tyrant, and detested by his people, became alarmed immediately, for he feared he would lose the throne. He summoned the Sanhedrin, the ecclesiastical council of the Jews, and inquired of them, "Where should Christ be born?" This question the Sanhedrin answered with ease. The prophecy was quite explicit on this point. The answer was "Bethlehem." Sending for the Wise Men, Herod gave them this information and cunningly told them to report back to him later, so that he too might adore the new King.

Eventually the Wise Men located the humble dwelling of the Holy Family, acquired no doubt, when the visitors, who had come for the registration had gone back home. Oblivious of these humble surroundings, the Wise Men prostrated themselves in homage. They then presented their gifts, gold, frankincense and myrrh—frankincense, for this Child is God; gold, for He is King of Kings; myrrh, for He is man as well as God. After a short stay the Wise Men, warned by God of Herod's hypocrisy, disappeared as mysteriously as they had come.

The respect and adoration of the Wise Men, contrasted with the hatred and hypocrisy of Herod, furnishes us with an early indication of what the Child Jesus will find, when later He begins to establish His Kingdom. His own townsfolk of Nazareth will spurn Him and attempt to stone Him to death. The Scribes and the Pharisees will lay traps for Him as He teaches, and unceasingly try to discredit Him with their duplicity. The chief priests and the elders will plot and scheme till, dredging the depths of injustice, they accomplish His death.

This lack of understanding shown Him by His own people was a greater trial for Christ than any physical suffering He had to bear. We may find, when under great stress, that those nearest us understand our suffering least. At such times, let us remember that no human understanding can give us the kind of help we most need. From Our Divine Master alone can we obtain the understanding and strength that will truly lighten our burden.

THE ADORATION OF THE WISE MEN by Peter Paul Rubens

The Flight into Egypt

Though thwarted for the moment, Herod's cruel designs spelled great danger for the Divine Child. The very night of the departure of the Wise Men, an angel appeared to Joseph in a dream and bade him fly with Christ and His mother into Egypt. The command was as urgent as the danger. Joseph, always obedient, gave instant compliance. After six or seven days of exhausting travel, Memphis was reached, where, tradition tells us, they settled for the duration of their stay in Egypt.

By this incident in Christ's life we are reminded that Jesus, Mary and Joseph had worry and suffering from His earliest days on earth. When trials and sufferings come to our own family, our greatest help is in learning from Christ's family how to accept and bear these sufferings. Complete trust in God and resignation to His will can enable our family to accept and overcome the greatest of sorrows.

Meanwhile, impatient at the failure of the Wise Men to return, Herod became more convinced than ever that the whole thing was a plot to dethrone him. In a characteristic blind rage, he formed his unspeakable plan. Sending for the soldiers of his guard, he ordered them to massacre all male children, two years old and under, in Bethlehem and its surrounding area. This measure, he felt, would certainly eliminate the Child who was a threat to his throne. The cruel command was swiftly carried out and the children shed their blood in martyrdom for the Cause of Christ.

Bethlehem and its environs would at this time have roughly two thousand people. If we take the usual ratio of thirty births annually per thousand, nearly equally divided between the two sexes, we obtain a figure of fifteen male children for one year, thirty for two years. Regardless of proportions this was a horrible crime, and treated as such by the Gospel narrative, which emphasizes it as one of the most bitter scenes in Jewish history, quoting the prophecy concerning Rachel's lamentation for her children; that voice in Rama which "would not be comforted because they are not."

A short time after his hideous crime, Herod, tormented by disease, died in agony. His people rejoiced at their deliverance and those who had fled to escape his cruelty began to return home. One cannot help but see in the agonizing death of Herod the avenging hand of God, and the pathetic futility of a mere creature attempting to frustrate the divine purpose.

Herod thus removed, the angel reappeared to Joseph, and directed him to take the Child and His mother back to Palestine. So the Holy Family returned from exile and settled in Nazareth.

THE FLIGHT INTO EGYPT by Bernhard Plockhorst

The Hidden Life of Jesus

THE DIVINE plan for Jesus, when the Holy Family had returned from exile and settled in Nazareth, was that He should lead a hidden life. In sharp contrast to the many wonders of His infancy, the succeeding years were to be wrapped in almost complete silence.

The Gospel story reminds us however of His unique status by unveiling an episode of the boyhood of Jesus. As pious Jews, Mary and Joseph made the annual pilgrimage to Jerusalem to celebrate the solemn feast of the Pasch. This episode concerns the pilgrimage made by the Holy Family when Jesus was twelve years old.

After the celebration of the feast, which lasted for a week, when the caravan was about to start on the return journey, Mary and Joseph discovered that Jesus was missing. Amidst the noise and bustle of the caravan preparing to leave, they inquired anxiously of Him. He might be with their relatives or friends. But the caravan was under way now and still there was no sign of Him. Sorrowfully, they decided to make the return journey to Jerusalem to search for Him there. At last, on the third day, they found Him in the Temple, sitting amongst the doctors, and astounding them with His wisdom. Before Him, in a semi-circle, sat the venerable rabbis craning forward in their eagerness as this young Boy so masterfully took charge of the discussion. The Talmud assures us that such discussion was common. But a boy of twelve, questioning and answering with such a depth of wisdom was indeed unique. With complete composure and no trace of shyness Jesus expounded the Scriptures with a clarity and understanding startling to these men who had a lifetime's training and experience in this very subject.

Perplexed by the whole incident, first by the sudden disappearance of so dutiful a son, now by finding him in such a scene, His mother gently asked for an explanation, telling Him of the sorrow and anxiety that had been caused Joseph and herself. In answer, Jesus simply reminded His mother that He was performing a task allotted Him by His Father in heaven; and of the many things He must do as Teacher of mankind.

Mary was not given a full explanation of Christ's reasons or plans. But her humility taught her to enquire no further. God does not choose to reveal His reasons or the details of His plans for our lives. Humility would teach us that we are, after all, only creatures and that our poor plans are very unimportant in comparison with the designs of our Creator, who truly wills our greatest good.

Jesus then obediently returned with them to Nazareth, where, for the next eighteen years, He was subject to them.

JESUS AT TWELVE by Heinrich Hofmann

The Coming of John the Baptist

Throughout their whole history the Jews clung to their great hope, the promise of the Savior. This was the cornerstone of their culture, their support in the midst of all the trials and tribulations witnessed by their race. Again and again their prophets had foretold it. They knew the poetry of the prophecies by heart, telling of the herald who would come before the King, preparing His way. "The voice of one crying in the wilderness. Prepare ye the way of the Lord."

John the Baptist was well known to many. His father was a prominent man and the circumstances of John the Baptist's birth were still remembered. His life as a hermit was in itself a fascination to people. Now he had emerged from his solitude and preached the coming of Christ, in fulfillment of his role as herald bearing witness of the Light through Whom all men might believe.

Many came to listen to him as a curiosity. Others were resentful of this unconventional figure. Gradually they found that his words gave life to their religion, and exposed much of it for what it was, empty convention. The Pharisees and Sadducees, religious leaders, impressed by his growing popularity, sought his favor. Well aware of their hypocrisy, he rejected their overtures.

After the harvest season, probably in October, we find Jesus emerging from His hidden life. The news of John the Baptist's preaching had reached Galilee, and a group set out along the Jordan on their way to hear him. One member of this group was Jesus, known to His townsmen as a carpenter. At the Jordan ford He, with the others, stopped to listen. With these others, unassuming as ever, He stepped forward to be baptized, last of the group. John the Baptist did not at first know who He was, so perfect was Our Lord's humility. Yet, even before God revealed it to him, he knew that this Man should be the one baptizing. This was the One for whom he was herald. Our Lord, however, meek and humble, overcame his protests and insisted on being baptized.

More and more we marvel at the humility of Christ. He was submissive to His Father's will in all things. As our Model, this, above all, He tried to teach us. Learning this lesson from Christ, whatever our problems or suffering, we prepare a way for God to enter our hearts with all His healing powers.

Showing submission on his part, His herald obeyed. After the baptism, when Jesus had stepped from the water, the Holy Spirit descended on Him in the form of a dove, and a voice from heaven said, "This is my beloved Son in whom I am well pleased."

THE BAPTISM OF JESUS by Christian Dalsgaard

The Samaritan Woman

AFTER HIS baptism, Our Lord went to a desert region and remained there fasting and praying for forty days. The hidden life was over. Now He prepared for His public life amongst His people. Satan, aware of approaching salvation through Christ, must use every weapon in his armory to stave off defeat. Jesus answered his temptations with a declaration of war, and sent him scurrying to defeat.

Two months after His baptism the Master's ministry began. One day, walking by the side of the Jordan He met John the Baptist who proclaimed Him "Lamb of God." Next day Jesus returned, and again John the Baptist proclaimed Him: "Behold the Lamb of God," and two of his disciples, Galileans, rose and followed Christ. Turning to them, Our Lord said, "What seek you?" Spontaneously, they answered "Rabbi," indicating that they accepted Him as their Master.

Next day, Andrew, who was one of the two, brought back Simon his brother. Before he could be introduced Jesus said, "Thou art Simon the son of Jona. Thou shalt be called Cephas." In this way Andrew and Simon, or Peter, became the first two disciples. Very soon, Philip and Nathanael joined them, and later the rest of the Twelve.

All was now ready. Now the Master would go forth to teach. He chose as the scene of His first public miracle a wedding feast at Cana, where in answer to His mother's request He changed water into wine. Proceeding from Cana to Jerusalem, He showed His authority by driving the money changers from the Temple, thereby incurring for the first time the wrath of the Scribes and Pharisees.

A year had passed and Christ continued to preach and baptize. The picture was not very bright, for though His followers had grown in number, Herod had thrown John the Baptist into prison, and the people of Judea had shown poor response to the Savior.

One day travelling through Samaria with His disciples, Jesus stopped by a well to rest. A Samaritan woman came to the well to draw water. Convention forbade His talking to her, but He asked her for a drink and conversed with her. Soon, through His gentle guidance, she confessed Him the Savior. This was farther than He had hitherto reached with anyone. She was "living in sin." But she had the heart to love and trust. She ran to her village, and broke the news. The people flocked to see and hear Him and many of them believed.

In Christ's gentle treatment of the Samaritan woman, we see the depths of His understanding. Any one in trouble had only to talk to Him to receive His sympathetic help. He asked only faith, to kindle hope and joy where everything had seemed impossible before. When sadness weighs on us heavily, let us take it to Him for help, trusting in His love and complete understanding.

JESUS AND THE SAMARITAN WOMAN by Carl Bloch

Sermon on the Mount

AFTER HIS two days in Samaria, Our Lord set out for His home town of Nazareth. On the way, he passed through Cana where He cured the ruler's son. In Nazareth He sadly discovered that indeed no prophet is accepted in his own country, for His townsmen, accusing Him of blasphemy, sought only to destroy Him. He escaped, however, to Capernaum (Capharnaum), a little town by the sea of Galilee, which became very dear to Him. Here He settled and worked many miracles. In this town He proved His claim of having the power to forgive sins by curing the paralytic. Soon the crippled and diseased constantly flocked around Him, exhausting Him with their endless entreaties. In His Manhood, He needs rest. So embarking on a small boat at Bethsaida, the disciples and He sought peace and quiet on the lake. Shortly afterwards, He appointed His twelve apostles who would preach and heal and cast out devils.

The crowds returned and there on the hillside rising from the lake He preached the Sermon on the Mount.

In this great Sermon, Christ taught us His Golden Rule—love God and thy neighbor for His sake. When gripped by the self-pity that accompanies set-backs and afflictions let us remember that many, in similar circumstances, have proved, by practicing the Golden Rule, that they can lose their own heartache in helping others bear their sorrows.

Mary Magdalene

ON THE RETURN journey to Capernaum from the Mount, Jesus, marvelling at a Roman Centurion's simple faith, rewarded him by healing his servant. Next day, in the neighboring town of Nain, He raised a widow's son from the dead. Later, in the fashionable town of Magdala, Our Lord again showed His love for those, who, though sinners, have a generous loving heart. Invited to the house of Simon the Pharisee, He was treated to a cold politeness so often extended to their guests by the snobbish rich. Suddenly a woman ran into the dining hall, and prostrated herself before Jesus in a welter of tears. With her hair she wiped His feet, and poured over them perfumed ointment. She was a notorious sinner whom no "respectable" person would allow near. Love is best expressed in deeds and Christ called attention to His treatment by this woman compared with the frigid hospitality He had been receiving.

Christ shows us always that deeds prove love. Lengthy misery over the misfortunes of a loved one really only proves our concern for ourselves rather than sympathy. Courage and constructive help, not tears, prove our love.

JESUS LOVES THOSE WHO LOVE by Anton Dorph

Jesus Calms the Storm

As was his practice, when exhausted by His labours, Our Lord sought a few hours peace on the lake. The fishermen amongst His disciples had boats lying on the shore. Soon they had one ready for the Master and were pulling out from shore towards Gerasa on the opposite side of the lake.

Suddenly a storm blew up threatening to capsize their small craft. The Master lay asleep, untroubled. His apostles were in panic. They frantically wakened Him, and He immediately quelled the storm. Then He chided them for their poor faith, again reminding them that His followers needed before all else a strong and firm faith in the Master.

At times, in life, we feel like a small flimsy craft being buffeted by the waves of sorrow and stress. Almost overcome by trials and difficulties, we want only to sink beneath life's waves. But the most dangerous storm is the one within our breasts. If we put our trust in God, He will bring His calm to our troubled hearts.

Next morning, they put in at Gerasa where He drove out the unclean spirit sending it into a herd of swine. Scarcely rested, they re-crossed the lake and returned to His beloved Capernaum. More miracles were to come. He cured the woman with the issue of blood and raised the daughter of Jairus to life. Now His fame was widespread throughout the countryside; nevertheless, when He returned to Nazareth, He found His townsmen still rejected Him. Nazareth would never be given another opportunity.

Another tour of Galilee served to show the disciples the fields white for the harvest and to prepare them for the work that lay ahead. Having instructed them, Our Lord sent them forth to teach and preach in the cities while He returned to Capernaum to pray for them. On His journey He received the sad news of John the Baptist's beheading by Herod. What suffering must have flooded His heart, for not only did He know that John alone amongst men fully understood Him and His work, but also that this marked the opening of warfare on Himself.

Soon, the Twelve returned, bubbling with enthusiasm in their accounts of their work. How they must have looked forward to the Master's commendation and further advice. But once more the crowds pressed, and to escape them they took ship to a desert place to rest. But there was no escape. The crowds followed the sail to meet Him where He landed. His heart touched by this devotion, He came ashore and taught them. Here He worked the miracle of the loaves and fishes. Thwarting their efforts to make Him king, Our Lord bade the apostles to take ship for Bethsaida, while He dismissed the people. That night, again showing them the importance of faith, He came walking over the water to join them as they sailed.

JESUS AND THE FISHERMEN by Ernst Zimmermann

The Transfiguration

THE GOSPEL accounts tell of the many miracles worked by Christ as He continues to journey about the countryside preaching His message. Despite His knowledge of the suffering and death that lay before Him there was a firm note of confidence in His preaching. Love and self-denial were the qualities required in anyone who would follow Him.

From the outskirts of Capernaum His little band moved southward to Mount Tabor (Thabor). Taking Peter, James and John, He climbed the steep slopes to the summit, and went aside to pray. His companions, though well intentioned, but weary with the climb, fell asleep. But soon they were awakened. They had made their ascent in the evening, and by now it was night, yet around them glowed light brighter than day. Focusing their eyes with difficulty, they saw that the light came from the spot where Jesus had knelt down to pray. But now a figure stood there. It was Jesus, yet he looked so different! The light coming from Him was as brilliant and blinding as the light from the sun. Though dazzled by the sight, they gradually perceived that Christ was conversing with Moses and Elias. Then it was all over. Jesus touched them, melting their fear and awe. Then they began the descent to rejoin the others.

Meanwhile, the other nine apostles had had a disappointing time. They had tried to cure a demoniac boy and had failed. Jesus instructed the boy's father that all things are possible to him who believes, and in response to the father's belief the son was cured. Then He patiently taught His disciples that their faith must be yet firmer, and that often there was need of prayer and fasting to carry out their work of healing.

Thence He passed on secretly to Galilee. After many months in Galilee, spent in training His disciples, He once more set out for Capernaum. Settled here, He had the time to continue His training of the Twelve. But not for long, for His work had to be resumed. Though humanly shrinking from it, He had to go up to Jerusalem for the Feast of the Tabernacles. Now the last battle was about to start, closing with His death and resurrection. Tiresome argument with doubters and hypocrites awaited Him in Jerusalem. Debate and argumentation are futile. Love and belief is what He asked.

These two qualities, faith and love, sum up everything we need to live as Christ taught us to live. Believing deeply in God, and loving Him above all else, there is no calamity in our lives that can shake us. For, as Job proved, the greatest of human afflictions need not rob us of our love of God and belief in Him; and with these intact we will surmount any misfortune.

JESUS ASKED LOVE AND BELIEF by Heinrich Hofmann

The Good Shepherd

During this stay in Jerusalem the Pharisees and His other enemies used every trick to trap Him. They brought to Him a woman accused of adultery, knowing His merciful treatment of such people. Citing the law of Moses they asked what His sentence would be. He quietly told them, "He that is without sin among you let him first cast a stone." Baffled once more, they slunk away. Thus does Our Lord deal with insincerity. And so the endless argumentation continued. The Pharisees drove the gentle Jesus to label them as a "generation of vipers." At last, since they continued to avoid the issue, He declared His divinity, using the strongest possible emphasis, "Before Abraham was, I am." This was clear. Jesus Christ is God. They took up stones to stone Him to death, but Jesus escaped, for His hour had not yet come.

Before leaving Jerusalem, Our Lord cured the man who was born blind. Instead of leading to a change of heart, this miracle was only another occasion for the Pharisees to attempt once more to prove that Jesus was a fraud. Again truth prevailed.

At the close of this troubled week in Jerusalem, Jesus led His friends to a nearby hillside, and expounded the parable of the Good Shepherd. It was the latter part of the autumn, and the rainy season was fast approaching. The sheep were scattered over the bare hills, nibbling at the scanty pasture. Every evening the shepherd came and counted them, calling each by name as he gathered them into the folds for the night. In his little hut nearby he kept constant vigil to protect them against thieves and desert beasts. In this beautiful teaching the Master explains that He is the Good Shepherd, ready to lay down His life for us, His sheep. Others, who do not accept Him, are His sheep too, and these must be brought into the fold so that there be one fold and one Shepherd.

In the loneliness and desolation that trials and sufferings bring, Christ's deep solicitude for each of us, as brought out so tenderly in the parable of the Good Shepherd, is particularly uplifting. The help we can expect from Him in our trouble is emphasized by His assurance of His readiness to die for us. We have but to ask Him, with trust in our hearts, and He will anxiously come to our assistance now, comforting us in our sorrow.

When He left Jerusalem, we find that Our Lord moved from place to place so that it is hard to keep track of His whereabouts. We are told that during this period He chose seventy-two disciples to promote His teaching and sent them out on His work.

THE GOOD SHEPHERD by Bernhard Plockhorst

The Raising of Lazarus

WE ALL have special friendships and Our Lord was no exception. He cherished the close friendship He had with Lazarus and his two sisters Martha and Mary, and He often visited them in their home at Bethany. Lazarus had become ill and his life was despaired of. No one knew better than his sisters the healing powers of Jesus. And they had seen that mostly His miraculous cures were an answer to faith and confidence. Distraught, they sent a message to Him saying simply, "He whom thou lovest is sick." When He got the news, Our Lord seemed strangely uninterested, and merely observed that everything would turn out all right, and that the whole incident would provide an occasion for further glory to God.

The disciples were pleased at this reaction. They were at the moment working quietly in Perea and the Master was prudent in not risking any foolhardy trip into Judea. Suddenly, He told them to get ready to go to Bethany, for Lazarus, their friend, was dead. As they tried to point out to Him the risk involved in going back into that region, He observed to His disciples that He was going to raise Lazarus from the dead, not only because of friendship, but because further miracles were needed to strengthen their own faith.

As Jesus and the Twelve approached the house, so well-known to all of them, Martha, the practical one, came running to meet them. Coming up to Jesus she told Him in her businesslike way that Lazarus just would not have died had He been there; but, more important, since anything He asks of God will be granted, her brother can be raised to life again if Jesus so wills. Again we see that faith and trust the Master always rewards. Then Mary, hearing of His arrival, frantic in her love, ran to Him and characteristically threw herself at His feet, pouring out her grief. Profoundly touched, Our Lord Himself wept. But His grief was momentary, for His teaching was one of joy and hope.

They made their way to the tomb and Jesus began to pray to His Father in heaven. Then in a loud voice He said, "Lazarus, come forth." It was a stupendous moment. All around the sepulchre were entranced. Lazarus came walking out of the tomb, bound in the death shroud.

The raising of Lazarus, like all Christ's miracles, was accomplished by Him to sow faith in the hearts of men. Christ did not, while on earth, remove pain and death because He regarded them as evil things. Suffering, He taught, can indeed lead us to Him, if accepted in the right spirit. Even death, the climax of suffering, is not the end, but the beginning of a new life in His Kingdom.

THE RAISING OF LAZARUS by Carl Bloch

Jesus and the Children

THOUGH MANY believed through the miracle of the raising of Lazarus, many were still unconvinced. But the chief priests and Pharisees were afraid of Our Lord's mounting importance and influence. Caiaphas (Caiphas), high-priest of this year, presided at a council meeting to discuss the problem. They decided that the Romans would soon tire of strife and faction amongst the Jewish people, and restrict further what liberty was left to them as a subject people. The interests of the Jewish nation required that Jesus must die. On hearing the sentence, Jesus, with the Twelve, went to a quiet little town called Ephraim. Here He would hide meantime.

At length the day came for setting out on His last journey to Jerusalem. On His way through Galilee the multitudes flocked to Him once more, and He taught them and healed many sick. On the outskirts of a little town in Galilee, He cured the ten lepers. Only one came back to thank Him. He had showered favors on so many, during His life, yet gratitude had been so seldom returned.

We have already seen the limitless love of Our Lord for all His people. He was indeed all things to all men. He shed His love on the learned and the unlearned; the old and the young; the good and the sinners; the grateful and the ungrateful. Even with the hypocrites He showed enormous patience and would ask His Father to forgive all His enemies as He hung dying on the cross. This utter love and tenderness of Our Lord we see highlighted in the touching scene of Jesus and the children that took place on this last journey to Jerusalem.

A number of women pushed through the crowds to have Him bless their children. The Twelve, feeling very important, now that Jesus was popular with the people, coldly turned the mothers aside, telling them that the Master was much too busy with more important matters. Jesus noticed what was going on. Lovingly, He gathered the children to Him and gently embraced them. As they clung to Him in their love, He called the Twelve and sharply reproved them for trying to keep the children from Him. They might have saved themselves this reproof, for they had seen His love for the poor, straightforward, simple people, and His detestation of the scheming diplomacy of the worldly-wise. All He asked was a childlike sincerity and trust. "Suffer little children to come unto me . . . for of such is the kingdom of God."

SUFFER LITTLE CHILDREN TO COME UNTO ME by Bernhard Plockhorst

Palm Sunday

AFTER VISITING the home of Zacchaeus, the tax supervisor, Jesus proceeded to Bethany. Here He attended a banquet given in His honor by Simon the Leper, a man cured of this disease by Our Lord. During this banquet the everloving Mary Magdalene anointed His feet with expensive ointment. Judas' criticism that this was sheer extravagance the Master sharply rebuked.

Next morning, preparing to leave Bethany, Jesus sent two disciples to Bethphage to fetch Him an ass and its colt. Thus would His entry into Jerusalem fulfill the prophecy foretelling the coming of the King. He would be poor and riding on an ass.

Surrounded by the people of Bethany, He began the journey to Jerusalem. The excitement mounted rapidly as the procession approached the gate and crowds poured out to meet them. Palm tree boughs were ripped down and strewn on the road before Him, and the wildly enthusiastic throng shouted their praise and welcome. Orders had been published that Jesus be arrested on sight, but the priests cringed into the background. Such popular acclaim they had not reckoned with.

The Moneychangers Expelled

THE NIGHT following the triumphal entry into Jerusalem was spent quietly in Bethany. Next day Our Lord returned to the Temple. Two years before, at the Pasch, He had driven the traffickers from the sacred enclosure with a whip braided of cords. Since then these men had returned to their old ways, encouraged by the priests and the ancients. The moneychangers, seated at their tables, were again in their former places. Nearby were the sellers of doves for the sacrifices. The din of voices raised in bargaining rang out through the whole sanctuary.

Once more Jesus impressed His authority as He turned over their tables with His foot, and drove them before Him from the Temple courts. How dare they desecrate the house of God! "My house shall be called the house of prayer; but ye have made it a den of thieves."

In our times, business and concern with the things of this life are often allowed to occupy our lives to the exclusion of God and His worship. Many wise people thank God for sending them the sharp jolt of sorrow through which they began to take stock of themselves, and came to realize the folly of this way of life.

JESUS DRIVING MONEYLENDERS FROM THE TEMPLE by Carl Bloch

Render unto Caesar

RETURNING again to the Temple on Tuesday, Jesus resumed His teaching. Never before had His teaching been received with such popular enthusiasm, so that the chief priest and scribes felt more and more helpless. But at all costs they must attempt to quell His rising popularity, so again they questioned Him on the authority He now so openly assumed. Again Jesus was patient with them, and tried to show them their folly through parables. The parables they refused to apply to themselves, no matter how obvious Jesus made it that they were aimed directly at them. The hardness of their hearts He could not pierce, and they turned and walked away.

By this time, thoroughly alarmed, and growing more fearful by the hour, the Pharisees opened up a new line of attack. They would seek to embroil Jesus with the secular authority, and cause Him to antagonize the Roman Governor. Slyly, affecting that they had almost been won over, they asked Him, "Is it lawful for us to give tribute to Caesar?"

Compulsion to pay taxes to their Roman overlords rankled strongly with the proud Jews. Furthermore, as dutiful observers of the Law of Moses, should they not resist this ordinance? If Jesus told them not to pay taxes, the Romans would immediately deal with Him. If He told them to pay taxes, the Pharisees would point out that He was not a loyal Jew. Such was the dilemma that these men in their cunning hypocrisy posed for Our Lord.

He knew their trickery and insincerity; so their dilemma He would answer with subtlety, and avoid implicating Himself. He asked for a coin and was handed a penny or a denarius, a little silver coin worth about fourteen cents. Taking the coin in His hand, He asked them, "Whose image and inscription is this?" They answered "Caesar's." As He handed back the coin to its owner, Our Lord simply said, "Render therefore unto Caesar the things that are Caesar's and unto God the things that are God's."

His reply was short and to the point. It showed them that He had not been for a moment deluded by their assumed simplicity. He did not lose His temper with their finesse and paltry diplomacy. He simply called their bluff, and exposed their half-truths for what they were.

Christ taught that justice consists in rendering to each his due. Our life is from God, and to Him we must return it. Let us always remember that we will be responsible for the manner in which we have used not only the joys He has sent us, but the sorrows, too.

RENDER UNTO CAESAR by Anton Dorph

The Last Supper

THE SANHEDRIN, a council composed of chief priests, Scribes and elders, having now finally rejected Jesus, met that night in the house of Caiaphas. Christ's popularity constrained them to take Him secretly. Thus did Judas, the traitor, play into their hands by his offer to betray the Master. They agreed to pay him thirty shekels, about seventeen dollars, for his treachery.

Wednesday passed without incident. Early Thursday morning, the day of the Pasch, Jesus sent Peter and John to Jerusalem to find a room and prepare for the paschal meal, where He with the others joined them in the evening. Before the supper, the Master set them an example of humility by washing the feet of each. When the meal was over, Our Lord informed them that He knew that one of them would betray Him. Stunned by this news, each one frantically blurted out, "Is it I, Lord?" Judas, sitting near, attempting a pathetic bluff, asked the same question. Our Lord replied quietly, "Thou hast said it." Rejecting the Master's offer of repentance, Judas hurried out into the night.

Then Jesus fulfilled His promise to give His flesh and blood as our food and drink. He blessed and broke bread and giving it to them bade them eat it saying, "This is my body." Then He took the cup and giving thanks gave it to them with the words, "Drink ye all of this. For this is my blood of the New Testament which is shed for many for the remission of sins." In these words Our Lord linked forever the ceremony of the Last Supper with His glorious Sacrifice on Calvary.

Agony in the Garden

AFTER these things, Jesus predicted Peter's denial. At length they left the supper room and set out for Mount Olivet. Coming to Gethsemane, Jesus led the party to an olive grove. Selecting Peter, James and John, He took them with Him apart from the others. Though desiring their comforting presence, He withdrew to pray alone. Horrified in His human nature at the picture of His coming sufferings, a sickening mixture of sorrow, and frustration flooded His soul. He cried out to His Father for relief, but immediately qualified His prayer with submission, "Thy will be done," forever the Model for us in all suffering. There is no misery or vexation that will not be relieved in a heart that can still murmur, "Thy will be done."

During this phase an angel appeared to strengthen Him. Yet even with this help, so intense was the agony blood oozed forth from the pores of His body, and trickled to the ground. Returning to seek solace from them, He found Peter, James and John asleep. Sadly, He chided them, and went back to His prayer and agony. Later, He returned, and again found them asleep. Without a word He went back to face the third and last phase of the agony.

THE AGONY IN THE GARDEN by Heinrich Hofmann

The Arrest, and Peter's Denial

CALM and courageous once more after His agony, Jesus, hearing the approach of those who came to arrest Him, awoke the apostles. He told them that His hour was at hand and intimated that He was going to deliver Himself to them voluntarily. The rabble was made up of some members of the Sanhedrin with their servants and a number of Roman soldiers.

Judas, in utter duplicity, simulated friendship and greeted Jesus warmly. Our Lord would have none of his hypocrisy and rebuked him for his betrayal of "the Son of Man with a kiss." Turning from the traitor, He made it clear that He would make their job easy, for He intended to deliver Himself to them. That He gave Himself up to them voluntarily He made even more clear through a miracle. For immediately on His telling them that it was He whom they sought, all the would-be captors nearest Him fell to the ground. Then He allowed them to take Him and they bound Him roughly. Inflamed at this handling of the Master he loved, Peter took out a sword and slashed at one of His captors, Malchus by name, injuring his right ear. Jesus restrained the apostles, cautioning them against violence, and healed the injured ear.

Our Lord was then dragged off, to face the revolting farce that they referred to as a trial. They took Him first to Annas, a former high Priest, and father-in-law of Caiaphas, who was presently in office. Satisfied, Annas charged them to take Jesus to Caiaphas, where the legal travesty continued.

Meanwhile, what of Peter and the others? After Our Lord's arrest they had fled, but Peter, ashamed of his fear, soon returned and followed a short distance behind Christ's captors. John too came back and joined Peter at Caiaphas' palace. Inside the palace Peter was asked by a portress if he were not one of Christ's disciples. He said in reply, "I am not." Then he joined other servants warming themselves around a fire in the courtyard, where a maid-servant told him that he looked like one of the Twelve. Indignantly he denied it. Still standing by the fire, again he was asked by a servant the same question. This time he denied even knowing Jesus. An hour later some servants told him they were sure he was a follower of Jesus; his very speech gave him away. Peter swore vehemently that he did not know his Master. During these denials the unmistakable crowing of a cock was heard three times. Later, as Our Lord was led from the palace, He fixed on Peter a searching look. His heart crushed, Peter fled from the palace in distraction, and burst into bitter tears.

Peter wept bitterly in his sorrow. Even he did not realize the depths of Christ's sympathy and understanding, which later turned Peter's tears to joy. In the bitter tears of our own periods of desolation, let us avail ourselves of Christ's sympathy and love, gaining. His strength in our sorrow.

PETER'S DENIAL OF JESUS by Carl Bloch

Christ Before Pilate

At Caiaphas' palace the sham continued, with false witnesses adding their quota to the mockery. Jesus, calm and dignified throughout this tournament of falsity, announced quite categorically that He was the Savior, and truly the Son of God. That was all Caiaphas wanted. Calling a halt to the whole pretence, he asked for and obtained from the servile assembly a unanimous vote for the death sentence. Jesus was then taken to Pontius Pilate whose ratification of the sentence was needed.

Pilate was impressed by the dignified bearing of Christ. So he returned Him to the Sanhedrin, and said he saw no reason for their accusations. As he noted the fanatical clamor that his reply set off, Pilate's weakness reasserted itself, and he told them to take Jesus to Herod Antipas, King of Galilee, since the accused was a Galilean, hoping in this way to evade responsibility. Herod simply used this directive as an occasion for clowning and mockery. Jesus was dressed in a white robe, and, in hideous jest, was treated as a fool to entertain the court. Then He was sent back to Pilate.

The Governor, disappointed that he was once more saddled with the responsibility of a decision, told the growing crowd outside his residence that he would punish Christ and release Him, for He did not deserve to die. Strange and distorted justice! Then another thought occurred to him. In deference to Jewish custom, the Romans released a prisoner on the occasion of the paschal festival. So he offered the mob a choice between Barabbas, a murderer, and Jesus. This, he thought, was the way out. But the mob's choice was definite and persistent; it wanted Christ crucified.

Pilate, thereupon, turned Jesus over to his soldiers to be scourged. Revelling in their sadism, the vulgar legionnaires did not confine themselves to the laceration of the whip. In brutal sport, they plaited a crown of thorns and cruelly forced it down upon His head. Then, thrusting a reed into His hand, they made gross mockery of His claim to kingship. This was the Christ, torn, bruised, and bleeding, that Pilate finally presented to the mob for its verdict. Attempting to stir their pity, he let them look on Jesus, admonishing them, "Behold the man."

Let us, too, "behold the man," and ask ourselves if there is any sorrow like His sorrow. In our own distress, be it great or small, we selfishly think there could be no suffering greater than what we bear. Consider, however, the uncomplaining Christ who bore all this agony voluntarily, to atone for our sins. Through our suffering runs self-concern; through His shines love.

BEHOLD THE MAN by Bartolomé Esteban Murillo

The Crucifixion

THE PERSISTENT scream from the mob, "Crucify Him, Crucify Him," was their heartless reaction, as Pilate presented Him to them in this pitiful condition. Though convinced of His innocence, the spineless Governor pandered to their cruel whim and pronounced the formula of condemnation: "Thou shalt go on the cross."

As was the custom, the execution of the sentence would take place immediately. The sorry procession was formed, a centurion leading the way, next a herald, announcing the reason for condemnation, then Our Lord, bent over, as He stumbled along with the heavy cross on His back.

The hill of Calvary is about a thousand yards from Pilate's residence, and fearing Jesus would collapse from exhaustion before getting there, the soldiers seized a man named Simon the Cyrenian and forced him to carry the cross. On the way, a group of women, overcome by sorrow, publicly sobbed as He passed by. Jesus, touched by their tears, turned to them, and softly, in a voice blurred with weakness, told them to keep their grief for themselves and their children, referring to the dreadful destruction that would descend on Jerusalem.

Even at this time of supreme suffering, Christ turned His thoughts to the grief of others. No one can know sorrow as He knew it and no one can understand our grief as He. It is good for us to recall that when cast down in sorrow we are especially dear to Him. We have only to ask and He will melt our grief in the fire of His love.

The insult and debasement of Our Lord, the King of Kings, as He was prodded and shoved along on this horrible journey, in a welter of blood and suffering, defies description. When Calvary had been reached, Jesus was offered, in accordance with ancient custom, a stimulant concocted of wine and myrrh. This small concession He would only touch with His bruised and parched lips. His bloodstained garments were ripped off; He was placed on a wooden stool and His hands nailed to the transverse bar of the cross. Then they nailed His feet. Words could not tell, nor would the sorrow welling in our hearts allow us to dwell on these things, nor on the frightful wretchedness endured by our gentle Christ during the next six long hours. His sufferings horrify us and we must turn our minds to His compassion. As they drove in the nails, He did not scream with anguish, as His human nature prompted Him to do. He had taught consistently forgiveness of enemies. In this supreme test that is exactly what He did. His only words were, "Father, forgive them, for they know not what they do."

The extreme of physical agony was not His only suffering. He had to witness the utter misery of His mother as the sword, foretold by Simeon, pierced her heart.

On all sides a somber curtain of agony misted His eyes. Jesus, our God, was dying.

THE CRUCIFIXION by Carl Bloch

Jesus Dies on the Cross

As our Savior hung dying on the cross, the soldiers, as was their grisly right according to law, cast lots for His garments. This settled, they took up guard duty at the foot of the cross, to which had been affixed in Latin, Greek and Hebrew, the inscription: "Jesus of Nazareth, the King of the Jews." In a pitiful attempt at sarcasm, Pilate had planned this as a humiliation for the Jews, as though further humiliation were possible after deicide.

The two brigands, crucified on either side of Christ, mingled their mockery with that of the others. They reminded Him of His claim of being able to rebuild the Temple in three days—of His saving others, and contemptuously told Him He now could not save Himself.

Suddenly, however, one of them turned to Christ, and contritely asked Our Lord to remember him when He shall come as King. The dying Jesus, returning kindness for insult, gently replied, "This day thou shalt be with me in paradise."

Ever a loving Son, Our Lord's thoughts were with His mother. Each pang of grief she suffered He shared with her. Solicitous for her well-being, He committed her to the care of His beloved disciple, John.

About noon, the heavens marked their disapproval and cast over the dreadful scene a curtain of gloom, which continued till three o'clock. Shortly before that fatal hour, His entire human nature rose in final distress, and a cry of utter agony escaped from His lips, "My God, My God, why hast thou forsaken Me?" No words could better portray the extremity of Our Lord's sufferings.

How consoling for us to know that even Christ, in His human nature, could be tempted to despair! In His agony, He cried out, "My God, my God, why hast thou forsaken me?" But then through the mists of pain He fought off this temptation and commended His soul to His Father. Under suffering's siege we, too, must commend ourselves to God.

Burning with fever, Christ gasped, "I thirst," and a bystander took a sponge, dipped in a mixture of vinegar and water, and fastening it to a branch of hyssop held it up to His mouth. His lips thus moistened, He indicated that His work on earth has been accomplished and that He is now ready to die. Quoting the Psalms, He uttered His last words, teeming with love of His Father till the end. "Father into thy hands I commend my spirit." Then with a final cry of pain, His outraged humanity reached the limit of endurance, and Our Savior, Victim for our sins on the altar of the cross, bowed His head and died.

SOLDIERS CASTING LOTS FOR THE GARMENT OF JESUS by James J. J. Tissot

The Resurrection

THE MOSAIC LAW stipulated that a corpse, after execution, be not left overnight; so the Sanhedrin, ever observant of the letter of the Law, petitioned Pilate to issue a command that the legs of those who hung on the cross be broken to hasten their death. The soldiers who came to carry out this order found Jesus already dead. One of them, however, to make sure, drove his spear into Our Lord's right side, and from the gaping wound there streamed a mixture of blood and water.

Before anything further could be done with the Sacred Body, Joseph of Arimathaea, loyal to Jesus though a member of the Sanhedrin, used his influence to obtain from Pilate permission to take charge of the dead Christ. Then Nicodemus and he, with profound respect, performed their sad task of taking the Master's body from the cross, and the sad little group, amongst whom was His mother, prepared the remains for burial. The body was washed and wrapped in bandages, which had been sprinkled with aromatic spices, and covered with a shroud provided by Joseph of Arimathaea. To this man also went the honor of offering a tomb, located only a few yards from Calvary. Then the small funeral procession, His mother, the holy women, and a few disciples, took the body to this sepulcher and Jesus was buried.

Next day, the Sabbath, all was quiet. Early on the following morning a group of devoted women, led by Mary Magdalene, hastened to the tomb, hoping to find someone to help them roll back the stone, for they intended to lavish further care on the Master's dead body. On their arrival, they found the stone rolled back and the soldiers lying terrified on the ground. Afraid and astonished, they were told by an angel that Jesus was not there, but had risen, as He said He would, and that they were to go and inform Peter and the others that the Master had gone into Galilee. Mary Magdalene, however, as soon as she had seen the door of the tomb lying open, had surmised that someone had taken the body. Immediately, she had turned and fled to bear word to Peter and John. On receiving this news they hurried to the sepulcher. Peter boldly entered first, and saw the bandages and shroud carefully folded and laid aside. Then John came in and looked around the empty tomb; in the words of Scripture, "He saw and believed."

Christ's resurrection is the climax and final triumph of His life on earth. His conquest of sin is victory over suffering and death—the legacy of sin. Here is the very essence of Christ's message. In Him and through Him we, too, conquer suffering and death, and turn all life's trials into ultimate triumph.

THE RESURRECTION by Carl Bloch

The Ascension

SHORTLY after Christ had risen from the dead He appeared to Mary Magdalene. At first she thought He was the gardener and, overcome with grief, pleaded with him to tell her where her dead Master's body had been taken. Then the Savior spoke one word, "Mary." It was enough. Her soul overflowing with faith, love and joy she threw herself at His feet crying out, "Master."

On Sunday afternoon two disciples were on their way from Jerusalem to the village of Emmaus. As they walked along discussing the distressing events of the last few days Jesus joined them. But they did not recognize Him. When they reached Emmaus Jesus accepted their invitation to join them in a meal. Breaking bread, He handed a piece to each. As soon as He had done so the disciples realized that their companion was Jesus; but before they could say a word the Master disappeared.

As the two disciples who had returned from Emmaus and joined the others at Jerusalem excitedly recounted their experience, Jesus joined the group and showed them the wounds in His hands and feet. Eight days later, He returned to rebuke Thomas, absent on the previous occasion, for insisting that he must touch the very wounds before believing that the Master had risen.

Later the apostles left Jerusalem and went to Galilee. One evening, Peter, with six other apostles, set out to fish on the lake. All night they fished, but caught nothing. At dawn, they saw a stranger on the shore, and when they had pulled near, this man told them to cast their net on the other side of the boat. They did so, and immediately made such a catch that they could not raise the net. At once Peter recognized Him, and crying out to the others, "It is the Lord," jumped into the water with his usual impetuosity, and swam the hundred yards to the shore.

In a happy reunion they built a little fire, made a meal at His invitation, and then settled down to hear the Master's words. He took this occasion to continue their training for the commission He had given them to "teach all nations, baptizing them in the name of the Father, and of the Son, and of the Holy Ghost." This training the Holy Spirit would complete on Pentecost.

At the appointed time, Our Lord's devoted followers went to Jerusalem, and were met there by the Master, who imparted to them His final instruction. His last words uttered, Jesus Christ, true God and true man, whose birth was a miracle, left the earth also in miraculous fashion. With His mother, the apostles, disciples, and holy women gathered round Him on Mount Olivet, He bade them farewell, and, as He blessed them, rose in great majesty till a cloud hid Him from sight.

CHRIST ASCENDS INTO HEAVEN by Andreas Herman Hunnaeus

This Story

MASTERPIECES of Christian art and simple prose have combined in unfolding this Life of Christ. This Story now stands before our minds in all its breadth and beauty, vividly depicting our Master and Model. But we alone can add depth to it.

Other stories are admired and praised and left there. This Story has to be carried always before our minds. The depth of inspiration "Come Unto Me" holds for us will be found when we learn its message and live its meaning. Only when that faith and love taught by Christ has saturated all our living can we gain the full measure of solace this Story offers. It is rather like a mirror in which, through constant gazing, we begin to discern there our own likeness, a likeness that sharpens and grows to the point where we can say with the Apostle Paul, "Christ liveth in me." More and more our selfishness and pride recede from the picture, yielding place to that love, humility and self-denial so beautifully portrayed for us in the life of the Master. The more we love God and hate sin, the more do we see our own image reflected from the Life of Christ.

With God's help and our own efforts we can constantly strive to see our own image in "Come Unto Me" as we allow the likeness of Christ to shine through us in all we do. Judging as He would judge, forgiving as He would forgive, loving as He would love, we will discover the courage, hope and consolation that provide the only true answer to life's "slings and arrows of outrageous fortune."

Thus can we win the deep spiritual strength that will control whatever distress may come our way, and will channel a pathway into our hearts for the peace of Christ. For His Wisdom teaches us that this earthly life, with all its trials and heartaches, is but a test. Life, therefore, can hold for us only one true failure—the loss of heaven's eternal reward; and only one true success—the achievement of everlasting happiness.